A DUA GUIDE FOR UMRAH

Step-by-Step Instructions to Perform Umrah and Essential DUAs from the Quran & Sunnah to Elevate Your Spiritual Journey

RABIATU MUHAMMAD

Table of Contents

Introduction

A Spiritual Journey: Your Ultimate Guide to Dua for Umrah

Embarking on the sacred pilgrimage of Umrah is more than just a physical journey; it's a profound spiritual odyssey that touches the depths of your soul. Imagine standing in the heart of Makkah, amidst the throng of pilgrims, feeling the divine presence that has drawn millions before you. Each step you take, every prayer you utter, and every moment spent in reflection becomes a thread in the tapestry of your spiritual awakening. But to truly unlock the essence of this transformative experience, you need a guide that speaks to your heart and soul. Welcome to "Dua for Umrah: A Spiritual Journey."

This guide isn't just a collection of prayers; it's a companion that walks with you through the sacred rituals, helping you to connect deeply with your faith. Picture yourself in Ihram, the white garments symbolizing purity and equality, as you recite the powerful duas that have been whispered by countless pilgrims over centuries. Feel the surge of emotion as you perform Tawaf, circling the Kaaba, each round bringing you closer to Allah, your heart echoing with the prayers that have been passed down through generations.

"Dua for Umrah" is meticulously crafted to not only provide the essential supplications but to also immerse you in their profound meanings. Each dua is accompanied by heartfelt reflections and insights that will elevate your spiritual state, making your Umrah an unforgettable, soul-stirring experience. Whether it's the heartfelt plea for forgiveness at Mount Arafat or the humble supplication at the Well of Zamzam, this guide ensures that every prayer you recite resonates with your innermost feelings and desires.

Imagine the sense of peace and fulfillment as you stand in the sacred precincts of the Haram, your heart unburdened, your spirit uplifted. This guide aims to bring you that sense of serenity, helping you to forge a deep and personal connection with Allah. With "Dua for Umrah," every moment of your pilgrimage becomes a step towards spiritual renewal and enlightenment.

Prepare to embark on a journey that will transform your heart and soul. Let "Dua for Umrah: A Spiritual Journey" be your trusted companion, guiding you through the sacred rites with wisdom, compassion, and profound reverence. Your path to spiritual fulfillment begins here.

- Significance of Umrah

Umrah, often referred to as the "lesser pilgrimage," holds a place of immense spiritual significance in Islam. Though not obligatory like Hajj, it is a profound act of worship that carries with it immense rewards and benefits. Umrah serves as a means of purifying the soul, seeking forgiveness from Allah (SWT), and drawing closer to Him.

The journey of Umrah is symbolic of a Muslim's devotion and submission to Allah. It is a voluntary act that demonstrates a deep yearning to connect with the Creator, to seek His mercy, and to renew one's commitment to a life of piety and righteousness. The physical acts involved in Umrah, such as Tawaf (circling the Kaaba) and Sa'i (walking between the hills of Safa and Marwah), are imbued with historical and spiritual significance, reflecting the trials and triumphs of the prophets and the believers who came before us.

One of the most significant aspects of Umrah is its ability to erase past sins. The Prophet Muhammad (PBUH) said, "The performance of Umrah is an expiation for the sins committed between it and the previous one" (Sahih al-Bukhari). This Hadith underscores the immense spiritual cleansing that Umrah provides, offering a fresh start for the believer. It is a chance to repent sincerely, to leave behind the mistakes of the past, and to return home spiritually rejuvenated.

Moreover, Umrah brings Muslims from all over the world together in a display of unity and brotherhood. Regardless of race, nationality, or social status, all pilgrims stand equal before Allah, dressed in the simple garments of Ihram. This sense of unity and equality serves as a powerful reminder of the core Islamic values of humility, compassion, and community.

In essence, Umrah is not just a physical journey to the holy cities of Makkah and Madinah; it is a spiritual voyage that transforms the heart and soul, bringing the believer closer to Allah and reinforcing the bond of faith that unites the Muslim Ummah.

- Importance of Dua in Umrah

Dua, or supplication, is a fundamental aspect of the Islamic faith, and its significance is magnified during the sacred journey of Umrah. As a direct means of communication with Allah (SWT), dua allows believers to express their innermost thoughts, desires, and needs, seeking divine guidance, forgiveness, and blessings. In the context of Umrah, dua is not only a form of worship but also a powerful tool that enhances the spiritual depth of the pilgrimage.

Umrah is a journey of both the body and the soul, and dua serves as the lifeline that keeps the pilgrim spiritually connected to Allah throughout this sacred expedition. Each stage of Umrah—from the intention (niyyah) to the final rites—presents an opportunity to engage in heartfelt supplication. These moments of dua transform the pilgrimage from a series of rituals into a profound spiritual experience, as the pilgrim actively seeks Allah's mercy, protection, and guidance.

One of the key reasons dua holds such importance in Umrah is its role in reinforcing the pilgrim's intentions and sincerity. The act of reciting dua, whether during Tawaf (circumambulation of the Kaaba), Sa'i (walking between Safa and Marwah), or any other rite, serves as a constant reminder of the purpose of the journey: to seek closeness to Allah and to purify the heart. Through dua, the pilgrim acknowledges their dependence on Allah and reaffirms their commitment to the path of righteousness.

Dua also acts as a source of comfort and solace during the journey. The physical demands of Umrah can be challenging, but the spiritual strength derived from sincere supplication helps pilgrims overcome any difficulties they may encounter. It is through dua that pilgrims find peace and reassurance, knowing that they are under the protection and guidance of Allah.

Moreover, dua in Umrah is a means of obtaining immense rewards. The Prophet Muhammad (PBUH) emphasized the power of dua, stating, "Dua is the essence of worship" (Tirmidhi). The sacred atmosphere of Makkah and Madinah, where Umrah is performed, amplifies the potency of supplications, making it a time when prayers are more likely to be answered.

In summary, dua is an integral part of the Umrah experience. It deepens the pilgrim's spiritual connection with Allah, provides comfort and strength, and plays a crucial role in ensuring that the journey is not just a physical act but a transformative spiritual event. Through dua, the pilgrim's heart is purified, their faith is strengthened, and their soul is uplifted, making Umrah a truly blessed and meaningful pilgrimage.

- How to Use This Guide

This guide has been meticulously crafted to accompany you through every step of your Umrah journey, ensuring that you are spiritually prepared and equipped with the right supplications at the right moments. To make the most of this guide, follow these simple instructions:

1. Familiarize Yourself with the Structure:
    - The guide is organized into chapters that correspond to the different stages of the Umrah pilgrimage: from preparatory duas before your journey, to the specific prayers for Tawaf, Sa'i, and the final rites. Begin by reviewing the table of contents to get an overview of the flow of the guide.

2. Learn the Duas in Advance:
    - Before you embark on your journey, spend some time learning and memorizing the key duas listed in each chapter. Understanding the meaning and significance of these supplications

will allow you to recite them with greater sincerity and focus during your pilgrimage.

3. Use the Guide During Your Journey:

   - Carry this guide with you as a pocket reference while performing Umrah. The guide is designed to be easily accessible, with specific duas clearly marked for each rite. Whether you are about to begin Tawaf or preparing for Sa'i, you can quickly find the appropriate supplication to recite.

4. Reflect on the Meanings:

   - Each dua is more than just words; it carries deep spiritual significance. Take a moment to reflect on the meaning of each supplication as you recite it. This mindfulness will enhance your spiritual connection and help you internalize the experience.

5. Personalize Your Supplications:

   - While this guide provides the essential duas, feel free to personalize your supplications by adding your own prayers and requests. Umrah is a time for personal reflection and connection with Allah, so let your heart guide your words.

6. Review and Reflect After Completing Each Rite:

- After completing each stage of Umrah, take a moment to review the duas you have recited. Reflect on your experience, the feelings that arose during the rituals, and how the supplications impacted your spiritual state.

7. Use the Guide for Post-Umrah Reflection:

- The guide includes a conclusion section to help you reflect on your entire Umrah experience once you have completed the pilgrimage. Use this time to contemplate how the journey has transformed you and how you can maintain the spiritual momentum in your daily life.

By following these steps, this guide will not only assist you in performing the rites of Umrah correctly but will also help you to immerse yourself fully in the spiritual essence of the pilgrimage. May it serve as a valuable companion on your sacred journey, bringing you closer to Allah and enriching your Umrah experience.

Chapter 1:

Preparatory Duas for Umrah

Before embarking on the sacred journey of Umrah, it's essential to spiritually prepare through specific duas. These supplications include prayers for safe travel, protection during the journey, and a heartfelt intention (niyyah) for Umrah. These duas help set the tone for a blessed and spiritually fulfilling pilgrimage.

Before setting out on the sacred journey of Umrah, recite specific duas to seek Allah's blessings and protection. These include:

1. Dua for Intention (Niyyah):
   - "O Allah, I intend to perform Umrah, so make it easy for me and accept it from me."

2. Dua for Safe Travel:
   - "Bismillah, tawakkaltu 'alallah, la hawla wa la quwwata illa billah."
   - Translation: "In the name of Allah, I place my trust in Allah, there is no power or strength except with Allah."

3. Dua for Protection:
   - "Subhanalladhi sakhkhara lana hadha wa ma kunna lahu muqrinin, wa inna ila rabbina lamunqalibun."
   - Translation: "Glory to Him who has subjected this (vehicle) to us, and we could

never have accomplished this (by ourselves), and surely to our Lord, we must return."

Reciting these duas helps ensure that your journey begins with a sincere intention and under Allah's guidance and protection.

- Dua for Intention (Niyyah)

Before beginning your Umrah, it is essential to set a clear and sincere intention (niyyah) for the pilgrimage. The following dua is recited to express your intention to perform Umrah:

- Dua: "اللهم إني أريد العمرة فيسرها لي وتقبلها مني."

- Transliteration: "Allahumma inni ureedu al-'umrata fa-yassirha li wa taqabbalha minni."

- Translation: "O Allah, I intend to perform Umrah, so make it easy for me and accept it from me."

This dua signifies your commitment to undertake the sacred journey solely for the sake of Allah, seeking His pleasure and rewards. Reciting it with sincerity helps ensure that your Umrah is performed with the correct intention and devotion.

- Dua for Safe Travel

As you embark on your journey for Umrah, it's important to seek Allah's protection and blessings for safe travel. The following dua is commonly recited:

- Dua: "بِسْمِ اللَّهِ، تَوَكَّلْتُ عَلَى اللهِ، لا حَوْلَ وَلا قُوَّةَ إِلَّا بِاللَّهِ."

- Transliteration: "Bismillah, tawakkaltu 'alallah, la hawla wa la quwwata illa billah."

- Translation: "In the name of Allah, I place my trust in Allah; there is no power or strength except with Allah."

This dua invokes Allah's protection over you and your journey, placing your trust in His care and affirming that all power and strength come from Him alone. It is a powerful reminder of reliance on Allah as you begin your pilgrimage.

- *1.2 Duas During the Journey*

As you travel towards the holy cities for Umrah, it is important to continuously seek Allah's protection, blessings, and guidance through specific supplications. These duas help maintain a spiritual connection throughout the journey:

1. Dua for Protection During Travel:
   - **Dua**: "سُبْحَانَ الَّذِي سَخَّرَ لَنَا هَذَا وَمَا كُنَّا لَهُ مُقْرِنِينَ، وَإِنَّا إِلَىٰ رَبِّنَا لَمُنْقَلِبُونَ."
   - **Transliteration**: "Subhanalladhi sakhkhara lana hadha wa ma kunna lahu muqrinin, wa inna ila rabbina lamunqalibun."
   - Translation: "Glory to Him who has subjected this (vehicle) to us, and we could never have accomplished this (by ourselves), and surely to our Lord, we must return."

2. Dua Upon Entering a New City:
   - **Dua**: "اللَّهُمَّ بَارِكْ لَنَا فِيهَا وَارْزُقْنَا خَيْرَهَا، وَخَيْرَ أَهْلِهَا، وَنَعُوذُ بِكَ مِنْ شَرِّهَا، وَشَرِّ أَهْلِهَا."

- Transliteration: "Allahumma barik lana fiha wa-rzuqna khayraha, wa khayra ahliha, wa na'udhu bika min sharriha, wa sharri ahliha."

- **Translation**: "O Allah, bless us in this city, provide us with its best, and protect us from its evil and the evil of its people."

3. Dua for Comfort and Ease:

- **Dua**: "اللَّهُمَّ هَوِّنْ عَلَيْنَا سَفَرَنَا هَذَا، وَاطْوِ عَنَّا بُعْدَهُ".

- Transliteration: "Allahumma hawwin 'alayna safarana hadha, wa-twi 'anna bu'dahu."

- Translation: "O Allah, make this journey easy for us and shorten its distance for us."

Reciting these duas during the journey helps ensure that you travel with Allah's protection, blessings, and ease, keeping your heart and mind focused on the spiritual significance of your pilgrimage.

- Dua for Protection

Seeking Allah's protection during your journey is crucial for peace of mind and safety. Here is a recommended dua for protection:

- Dua: "أَعُوذُ بِكَلِمَاتِ اللَّهِ التَّامَّاتِ مِن شَرِّ مَا خَلَقَ".

-    Transliteration: "A'udhu   bikalimatillahi at-tammati min sharri ma khalaq."

- Translation: "I seek refuge in the perfect words of Allah from the evil of what He has created."

This dua is a powerful invocation for Allah's protection against all forms of harm and evil. Reciting it regularly during your journey helps ensure that you are under Allah's safeguarding and care.

- Dua When Entering a New City

Upon arriving in a new city, it is a tradition to seek Allah's blessings and protection. Here is a recommended dua for this moment:

- Dua: "اللَّهُمَّ بَارِكْ لَنَا فِي هَذِهِ الْمَدِينَةِ، وَارْزُقْنَا خَيْرَهَا وَخَيْرَ أَهْلِهَا، وَنَعُوذُ بِكَ مِنْ شَرِّهَا وَشَرِّ أَهْلِهَا."

- Transliteration: "Allahumma barik lana fi hadhihi al-madina, wa-rzuqna khayraha wa khayra ahliha, wa na'udhu bika min sharriha wa sharri ahliha."

- Translation: "O Allah, bless us in this city, provide us with its best, and protect us from its evil and the evil of its people."

This dua is meant to invoke Allah's blessings on the new environment and ensure safety and prosperity during your stay.

- *1.3 Duas Upon Reaching Makkah*

Upon arriving in Makkah, it's customary to recite specific duas to seek Allah's blessings and express your gratitude. Here are recommended duas for this sacred moment:

1. Dua Upon Seeing the Kaaba:
- **Dua**:" اللَّهُمَّ زِدْ هَاذِهِ الْبَلْدَةَ شَرَفًا وَتَعْظِيمًا وَبَرَكَةً، وَزِدْ مَنْ سَكَنَهَا مِنَ الْمُؤْمِنِينَ شَرَفًا وَعِزًّا."

- Transliteration: "Allahumma zid hadhihi al-baldata sharafan wa ta'zimam wa barakatan, wa zid man sakana fiha min al-mu'minina sharafan wa 'izzan."

- Translation: "O Allah, increase the honor, reverence, and blessings of this city, and increase the honor and dignity of the believers who reside in it."

2. Dua Upon Entering Masjid al-Haram:
- Dua: "اللَّهُمَّ افْتَحْ لِي أَبْوَابَ رَحْمَتِكَ، وَاغْفِرْ لِي ذُنُوبِي، وَارْزُقْنِي أَجْرَ الْعُمَرَةِ."

- Transliteration: "Allahumma iftah li abwaba rahmatika, waghfir li dhunubi, wa-rzuqni ajra al-'umrah."

- Translation: "O Allah, open for me the doors of Your mercy, forgive my sins, and grant me the reward of Umrah."

3. Dua for the Spiritual Experience:
- Dua: "اللَّهُمَّ إِنِّي أَسْأَلُكَ قَلْبًا صَافِيًا وَعَمَلًا صَالِحًا وَقُرْبًا مِنْكَ."

- Transliteration: "Allahumma inni as'alu ka qalban safiyyan wa 'amalan salihan wa qurban minka."

- Translation: "O Allah, I ask You for a pure heart, righteous deeds, and closeness to You."

Reciting these duas upon reaching Makkah helps you begin your Umrah with the right intentions, seeking Allah's blessings and guidance as you embark on this spiritual journey.

- Dua Upon Seeing the Kaaba

When you first see the Kaaba, it is a moment of profound spiritual significance. It is customary to make a special dua at this moment to express your awe and seek Allah's blessings. Here is a recommended dua:

- Dua: "اللَّهُمَّ زِدْ هَٰذِهِ الْبَيْتَ شَرَفًا وَمَجْدًا وَعِزًّا وَبَرَكَةً، وَمَنْ حَجَّهُ أَوِ اعْتَمَرَهُ فِي حَياتِي وَمَمَاتِي فِي خَيْرٍ".

- Transliteration: "Allahumma zid hadha al-bayta sharafan wa majdan wa 'izzan wa barakatan, wa man hajjahu aw i'tamara hu fi hayati wa mamati fi khayrin."

- Translation: "O Allah, increase the honor, glory, dignity, and blessings of this House, and grant goodness to those who perform Hajj or Umrah to it in my lifetime and after my death."

This dua reflects gratitude and reverence for the Kaaba, while also seeking Allah's blessings for those who come to it for worship.

- *Dua Upon Entering Masjid al-Haram*

When entering the sacred Masjid al-Haram in Makkah, it is recommended to recite a dua that expresses humility, reverence, and the hope for Allah's mercy and forgiveness. This dua sets the tone for the spiritual experience within the most revered mosque in Islam.

- Dua: "اللَّهُمَّ افْتَحْ لِي أَبْوَابَ رَحْمَتِكَ."

- Transliteration: "Allahumma iftah li abwaba rahmatika."

- Translation: "O Allah, open for me the doors of Your mercy."

Additional Duas Upon Entering Masjid al-Haram

1. Dua for Protection from Evil:
   - Dua: "أَعُوذُ بِاللَّهِ الْعَظِيمِ، وَبِوَجْهِهِ الْكَرِيمِ، وَسُلْطَانِهِ الْقَدِيمِ، مِنَ الشَّيْطَانِ الرَّجِيمِ."

- Transliteration: "A'udhu billahi al-'Azim, wa bi-wajhihi al-karim, wa bi-sultanihi al-qadim, min al-shaytan al-rajim."

- Translation: "I seek refuge in Allah, the Mighty, and in His noble countenance, and His eternal authority, from the accursed Shaytan."

2. Dua for Acceptance of Worship:
- **Dua**: "اللَّهُمَّ اجْعَلْ هَذِهِ الزِّيَارَةَ مَقْبُولَةً وَزَكِيَّةً".

- Transliteration: "Allahumma ja'al hadhihi al-ziyara maqboolatan wa zakiyyatan."

- Translation: "O Allah, make this visit accepted and pure."

3. Dua for Peace and Serenity:
- **Dua**: "اللَّهُمَّ اجْعَلْ دُخُولِي هَذَا دُخُولَ السَّلَامِ وَالْإِيمَانِ".

- Transliteration: "Allahumma ja'al dukhuli hadha dukhuul al-salam wa al-iman."

- Translation: "O Allah, make my entering this place an entry of peace and faith."

These duas help set a reverent and mindful tone as you enter Masjid al-Haram, ensuring that your time spent in this sacred place is filled with spiritual reflection and connection with Allah.

Chapter 2:

Duas for Tawaf

Dua Upon Entering Masjid al-Haram

Entering Masjid al-Haram, the holiest mosque in Islam, is a profound experience. It's customary to recite a special dua to seek Allah's blessings and forgiveness. Here is a recommended dua for this moment:

- Dua: "اللَّهُمَّ افْتَحْ لِي أَبْوَابَ رَحْمَتِكَ، وَاغْفِرْ لِي ذُنُوبِي، وَارْزُقْنِي أَجْرَ الْعُمَرَةِ."

- Transliteration: "Allahumma iftah li abwaba rahmatika, waghfir li dhunubi, wa-rzuqni ajra al-'umrah."

- Translation: "O Allah, open for me the doors of Your mercy, forgive my sins, and grant me the reward of Umrah."

This dua helps you enter the sacred mosque with a heart full of devotion, seeking Allah's mercy, forgiveness, and blessings as you commence your pilgrimage.

- 2.1 Duas for Each Round of Tawaf

Duas for Tawaf

During Tawaf, the ritual of circumambulating the Kaaba, specific duas can enhance the spiritual experience. Here are some recommended duas to recite while performing Tawaf:

1. General Dua for Tawaf:
- **Dua**:" اللَّهُمَّ اجْعَلْنِي مِنَ التَّوَّابِينَ وَاجْعَلْنِي مِنَ الْمُتَطَهِّرِينَ."

- Transliteration: "Allahumma ajilni min al-tawwabeen wa ajilni min al-mutatahhireen."

- Translation: "O Allah, make me among those who frequently repent and those who are purified."

2. Dua for Forgiveness and Mercy:
- Dua: "اللَّهُمَّ اغْفِرْ لِي وَارْحَمْنِي وَهْدِنِي وَارْزُقْنِي".

   - Transliteration: "Allahumma ghfir li wa irhamni wa hdini wa-rzuqni."

   - Translation: "O Allah, forgive me, have mercy on me, guide me, and provide for me."

3. Dua for Protection and Guidance:
- **Dua**: "اللَّهُمَّ احْفَظْنِي مِنَ الشَّرِّ وَالْفِتَنِ، وَاحْفَظْ عَائِلَتِي وَأَحِبَّتِي".

   - Transliteration: "Allahumma ihfazni min al-sharri wa al-fitani, wa ihfaz 'ailati wa ahibbati."

   - Translation: "O Allah, protect me from harm and trials, and safeguard my family and loved ones."

4. Dua at the Black Stone (Hajar al-Aswad):

- Dua: "بِسْمِ اللَّهِ وَاللَّهُ أَكْبَرُ."

- Transliteration: "Bismillah wa Allahu Akbar."

- Translation: "In the name of Allah, and Allah is the Greatest."

- Note: When you reach the Black Stone, it's customary to say "Bismillah" and "Allahu Akbar" while touching or pointing to it.

These duas help focus your heart and mind during Tawaf, seeking Allah's forgiveness, guidance, and protection while engaging in this central rite of Umrah.

- Specific Duas for Each Round

While performing Tawaf, the ritual involves circumambulating the Kaaba seven times. Each round can be an opportunity to make specific supplications or reflect on particular aspects of your faith. Here are suggested duas for each round:

1. First Round:
   - **Dua**: "اللَّهُمَّ اجْعَلْنِي مِنَ الْمُقَرَّبِينَ وَالْمُتَّقِينَ، وَاقْبَلْ عُمَرَتِي."

   - Transliteration: "Allahumma ajilni min al-muqarrabeen wa al-muttaqeen, wa-qabbil 'umrati."

   - Translation: "O Allah, make me among those who are brought close (to You) and the righteous, and accept my Umrah."

2. Second Round:
   - Dua: "اللَّهُمَّ اغْفِرْ لِي ذُنُوبِي وَسَوِّىٰ صَدْرِي."

- Transliteration: "Allahumma ghfir li dhunubi wa sawwi sadri."

  - Translation: "O Allah, forgive my sins and purify my heart."

3. Third Round:
  - Dua: "اللَّهُمَّ زِدْ هَـٰذِهِ الْبَيْتَ شَرَفًا وَمَجْدًا وَبَرَكَةً."

  - Transliteration: "Allahumma zid hadha al-bayta sharafan wa majdan wa barakatan."

  - Translation: "O Allah, increase the honor, glory, and blessings of this House."

4. Fourth Round:
  - **Dua**: "اللَّهُمَّ ارحَمْنِي وَرَحْمَتُكَ قَرِيبَةٌ مِنَ الْمُحْسِنِينَ."

  - Transliteration: "Allahumma irhamni wa rahmatuka qareebatun min al-muhsineen."

- Translation: "O Allah, have mercy on me, for Your mercy is near to the doers of good."

5. Fifth Round:
   - Dua: "اللَّهُمَّ اجْعَلْنِي مِنَ الصَّابِرِينَ وَالْمُؤْمِنِينَ."

   - Transliteration: "Allahumma ajilni min al-sabireen wa al-mu'minin."

   - Translation: "O Allah, make me among those who are patient and the believers."

6. Sixth Round:
   - Dua: "اللَّهُمَّ قَبِلْ تَوْبَتِي وَطَهِّرْ قَلْبِي."

   - Transliteration: "Allahumma qabill tawbati wa tahhir qalbi."

   - Translation: "O Allah, accept my repentance and purify my heart."

7. Seventh Round:
   - Dua: "اللَّهُمَّ اجْعَلْنِي مِنَ الْمُخْلِصِينَ لَكَ الدِّينَ وَسَلِّمْنِي مِنَ الْفِتَنِ."

- Transliteration: "Allahumma ajilni min al-mukhlisina laka al-dina wa sallimni min al-fitani."

- Translation: "O Allah, make me among those who sincerely dedicate their faith to You and protect me from trials."

These duas help maintain focus and sincerity during each round of Tawaf, allowing you to make specific supplications and reflections while performing this important ritual.

- 2.2 General Duas During Tawaf

During Tawaf, you can recite various general duas to seek Allah's blessings and enhance your spiritual experience. Here are some suggested general duas:

1. Dua for Forgiveness:
   - Dua: "اللَّهُمَّ اغْفِرْ لِي وَارْحَمْنِي وَاعْفُ عَنِّي".

     - Transliteration: "Allahumma ghfir li wa irhamni wa 'fu 'anni."

     - Translation: "O Allah, forgive me, have mercy on me, and pardon me."

2. Dua for Guidance:
   - Dua: "اللَّهُمَّ اهْدِنِي وَسَدِّدْنِي".

     - Transliteration: "Allahumma ihdini wa saddidni."

   - Translation: "O Allah, guide me and keep me steadfast."

3. Dua for Protection:
   - Dua: "اللَّهُمَّ احْفَظْنِي مِنَ الشَّرِّ وَالْفِتَنِ."

   - Transliteration: "Allahumma ihfazni min al-sharri wa al-fitani."

   - Translation: "O Allah, protect me from harm and trials."

4. Dua for Mercy and Blessings**:
   - Dua: "اللَّهُمَّ صَلِّ عَلَىٰ نَبِيِّنَا مُحَمَّدٍ وَبَارِكْ عَلَيْهِ."

   - Transliteration: "Allahumma salli ‘ala nabiyyina Muhammad wa barik ‘alayh."

   - Translation: "O Allah, send peace and blessings upon our Prophet Muhammad."

5. Dua for Righteous Deeds:
   - Dua: "اللَّهُمَّ اجْعَلْ عَمَلِي خَالِصًا لِوُجْهِكَ الْكَرِيمِ."

   - Transliteration: "Allahumma ajilni ‘amali khalisan liwajhika al-kareem."

- Translation: "O Allah, make my deeds sincere for Your noble sake."

6. Dua for Strength and Patience:
- Dua: "اللَّهُمَّ قَوِّنِي عَلَىٰ صَرْفِ أَوْقَاتِ التَّقْصِيرِ."

- Transliteration: "Allahumma qawwini 'ala sarfi awqat al-taqsiri."

- Translation: "O Allah, strengthen me to avoid times of neglect."

Reciting these general duas during Tawaf helps maintain a connection with Allah, seeking His forgiveness, guidance, and protection, and ensuring that your actions are performed with sincerity and devotion.

- Dua for Forgiveness Tawaf

During Tawaf, seeking forgiveness from Allah is a deeply meaningful aspect of the ritual. Here is a recommended dua for forgiveness that you can recite during your circumambulation of the Kaaba:

- Dua: "اللَّهُمَّ اغْفِرْ لِي ذُنُوبِي وَكَفِّرْ عَنِّي سَيِّئَاتِي، وَطَهِّرْ قَلْبِي."

- Transliteration: "Allahumma ghfir li dhunubi wa kaffir 'anni sayyi'ati, wa tahhir qalbi."

- Translation: "O Allah, forgive my sins and expiate my misdeeds, and purify my heart."

Reciting this dua during Tawaf helps you seek Allah's mercy and forgiveness while expressing a sincere desire for spiritual cleansing and renewal.

- Dua for Guidance and Protection During Tawaf

During Tawaf, seeking Allah's guidance and protection is essential for a spiritually enriching experience. Here is a dua for these purposes:

- Dua: "اللَّهُمَّ اهْدِنِي وَاحْفَظْنِي مِنْ كُلِّ شَرٍّ وَفِتْنَةٍ."

- Transliteration: "Allahumma ihdini wa ihfazni min kulli sharri wa fitna."

- Translation: "O Allah, guide me and protect me from all harm and trials."

Reciting this dua helps you seek Allah's direction and safeguarding, ensuring that your Tawaf is performed with a clear heart and under divine protection.

- *2.3 Duas After Completing Tawaf*

After completing Tawaf, it's beneficial to recite specific duas to seek Allah's blessings, express gratitude, and ask for further guidance. Here are some recommended duas:

1. Dua for Gratitude and Acceptance:
   - **Dua**: "اللَّهُمَّ تَقَبَّلْ عُمَرَتِي وَاغْفِرْ لِي وَارْحَمْنِي."

   - Transliteration: "Allahumma taqabbal 'umrati wa ghfir li wa irhamni."

   - Translation: "O Allah, accept my Umrah, forgive me, and have mercy on me."

2. Dua for Forgiveness and Mercy:
   - Dua: "اللَّهُمَّ اغْفِرْ لِي ذُنُوبِي وَسَوِّى صَدْرِي."

   - Transliteration: "Allahumma ghfir li dhunubi wa sawwi sadri."

   - Translation: "O Allah, forgive my sins and purify my heart."

3. Dua for Seeking Goodness and Blessings:
   - Dua: "اللَّهُمَّ اجْعَلْنِي مِنَ التُّقَاةِ وَالْمُقَرَّبِينَ".

   - Transliteration: "Allahumma ajilni min al-taqati wa al-muqarrabeen."

   - Translation: "O Allah, make me among the pious and those who are brought close (to You)."

4. Dua for Protection from Future Trials:
   - Dua: "اللَّهُمَّ احْفَظْنِي مِنْ كُلِّ شَرٍّ وَفِتْنَةٍ".

   - Transliteration: "Allahumma ihfazni min kulli sharri wa fitna."

   - Translation: "O Allah, protect me from all harm and trials."

These duas help you to conclude your Tawaf with a sense of spiritual fulfillment, seeking Allah's acceptance, forgiveness, and continued guidance.

- Dua of Istighfar

Istighfar, or seeking forgiveness, is a central aspect of worship in Islam. Reciting the following dua for Istighfar helps in seeking Allah's pardon and cleansing from sins:

- Dua: "أَسْتَغْفِرُ اللَّهَ رَبِّي مِن كُلِّ ذَنْبٍ وَأَتُوبُ إِلَيْهِ."

- Transliteration: "Astaghfirullaha rabbi min kulli dhambin wa atubu ilayh."

- Translation: "I seek forgiveness from Allah, my Lord, from all my sins, and I turn to Him in repentance."

This dua can be recited frequently, especially during moments of reflection and after performing acts of worship like Tawaf, to seek Allah's mercy and forgiveness.

- Dua at Maqam Ibrahim

When you visit Maqam Ibrahim (the Station of Ibrahim), it is customary to recite a specific dua. Maqam Ibrahim is the stone upon which Prophet Ibrahim (Abraham) stood while building the Kaaba. Here is a recommended dua to recite at this sacred site:

- Dua: "رَبِّ اجْعَلْ هَٰذَا بَلَدًا آمِنًا وَارْزُقْ أَهْلَهُ مِنَ الثَّمَرَاتِ".

- Transliteration: "Rabbij 'al hadha baladan aminan wa-rzuq ahlahu min al-thamarat."

- Translation: "My Lord, make this a secure city and provide its people with fruits."

This dua reflects the supplication of Prophet Ibrahim (AS) for the safety and sustenance of Makkah and its inhabitants. Reciting it helps to honor the legacy of Prophet Ibrahim and seek Allah's blessings for security and provision.

Chapter 3

- Duas for Sa'i (Between Safa and Marwah)

During Sa'i, the ritual of walking between the hills of Safa and Marwah, specific duas can enhance the spiritual experience. Here are some recommended duas:

1. General Dua for Sa'i:
   - Dua: "اللَّهُمَّ اجْعَلْ سَعْيِي هَٰذَا سَعْيًا مَقْبُولًا وَذُنُوبِي مَغْفُورَةً".

   - Transliteration: "Allahumma ajilni sa'yi hadha sa'yan maqbulan wa dhunubi maghfuratan."

   - Translation: "O Allah, make this Sa'i of mine accepted and my sins forgiven."

2. Dua for Seeking Blessings and Mercy:
   - Dua: "اللَّهُمَّ اجْعَلْ سَعْيِي مَغْفُورًا وَمُتَقَبَّلًا وَزِدْنِي مِنْ بَرَكَتِكَ".

- Transliteration: "Allahumma ajilni sa'yi maghfuratan wa mutaqabbilan wa zidni min barakatika."

- Translation: "O Allah, make my Sa'i forgiven and accepted, and increase me in Your blessings."

3. Dua for Fulfillment of Needs:
   - Dua: "اللَّهُمَّ اقْضِ حَاجَتِي وَارْزُقْنِي مِنَ الْخَيْرِ."

   - Transliteration: "Allahumma uqdi hajatihi wa-rzuqni min al-khayri."

   - Translation: "O Allah, fulfill my needs and provide me with goodness."

4. Dua for Spiritual Strength and Perseverance:
   - Dua: "اللَّهُمَّ قَوِّنِي عَلَىٰ سَعْيِي وَصَبِّرْنِي."

   - Transliteration: "Allahumma qawwini 'ala sa'yi wa sabbirni."

- Translation: "O Allah, strengthen me in my Sa'i and grant me patience."

These duas help you maintain focus and devotion while performing Sa'i, seeking Allah's blessings, forgiveness, and fulfillment of your needs.

3.1 Duas When Ascending Safa and Marwah

When ascending the hills of Safa and Marwah during Sa'i, it is customary to recite specific duas. Here are some recommended supplications:

1. Dua When Ascending Safa:
   - **Dua**: "اللَّهُمَّ اجْعَلْنِي مِنَ الْمُتَّقِينَ وَفِرْ لِي ذُنُوبِي وَاجْعَلْنِي مِنَ الصَّابِرِينَ."

   - Transliteration: "Allahumma ajilni min al-muttaqeen wa fir li dhunubi wa ajilni min al-sabireen."

   - Translation: "O Allah, make me among the pious, forgive my sins, and make me among the patient."

   - Note: At Safa, you should face the Kaaba and raise your hands in supplication, asking Allah for guidance, forgiveness, and blessings.

2. Dua When Ascending Marwah:

- Dua: "اللَّهُمَّ اجْعَلْنِي مِنَ الصَّالِحِينَ وَارْزُقْنِي خَيْرًا وَتَقَبَّلْ عُمَرَتِي."

- Transliteration: "Allahumma ajilni min al-salihin wa-rzuqni khayran wa taqabbal 'umrati."

- Translation: "O Allah, make me among the righteous, provide me with goodness, and accept my Umrah."

- Note: At Marwah, you should also face the Kaaba and make your supplications. This is an opportunity to ask Allah for your personal needs and desires.

These duas are recited while ascending Safa and Marwah, focusing on seeking Allah's blessings, forgiveness, and guidance during the Sa'i ritual.

- *Dua Upon Reaching Safa*

When you reach the hill of Safa during the Sa'i ritual, it is a time for supplication and reflection. Here is a recommended dua to recite upon reaching Safa:

- Dua: "لَا إِلَهَ إِلَّا اللَّهُ وَحْدَهُ لَا شَرِيكَ لَهُ، لَهُ الْمُلْكُ وَلَهُ الْحَمْدُ وَهُوَ عَلَىٰ كُلِّ شَيْءٍ قَدِيرٌ."

- Transliteration: "La ilaha illa Allah wahdahu la sharika lahu, lahu al-mulku wa lahu al-hamdu wa huwa 'ala kulli shay'in qadir."

- Translation: "There is no deity except Allah alone, with no partner. To Him belongs the dominion, and to Him is praise, and He has power over all things."

Additional Supplications

- General Dua for Guidance and Blessings:
- Dua: "اللَّهُمَّ اجْعَلْنِي مِنَ الْمُتَّقِينَ وَارْزُقْنِي مِنْ بَرَكَاتِكَ."

- Transliteration: "Allahumma ajilni min al-muttaqeen wa-rzuqni min barakatika."

- Translation: "O Allah, make me among the pious and provide me with Your blessings."

When at Safa, you should face the Kaaba, raise your hands if possible, and make personal supplications, seeking Allah's guidance, blessings, and forgiveness. This is a special time to express your heartfelt requests and gratitude.

- *Dua Upon Reaching Marwah*

When you reach the hill of Marwah during the Sa'i ritual, it is an important moment for supplication and reflection. Here is a recommended dua to recite upon reaching Marwah:

- Dua: "اللَّهُمَّ اجْعَلْنِي مِنَ الصَّابِرِينَ وَارْزُقْنِي خَيْرَ الدُّنْيَا وَالآخِرَةِ."

- Transliteration: "Allahumma ajilni min al-sabireen wa-rzuqni khayra al-dunya wa al-akhirah."

- Translation: "O Allah, make me among the patient and provide me with the best of this world and the Hereafter."

Additional Supplications

- General Dua for Success and Acceptance:
- Dua: "اللَّهُمَّ تَقَبَّلْ عُمَرَتِي وَاغْفِرْ لِي وَارْزُقْنِي مِنْ خَيْرِكَ."

- Transliteration: "Allahumma taqabbal 'umrati wa ghfir li wa-rzuqni min khayrika."

- Translation: "O Allah, accept my Umrah, forgive me, and grant me Your goodness."

As you reach Marwah, face the Kaaba if possible, raise your hands, and make personal supplications, asking Allah for guidance, blessings, and forgiveness. This is a special moment to seek Allah's favor and express your heartfelt needs.

- *3.2 Duas During the Walk*

During the walk between Safa and Marwah (Sa'i), you can recite various duas and supplications to enhance your spiritual experience. Here are some recommended duas:

1. Dua for Guidance and Forgiveness:
   - Dua: "اللَّهُمَّ ارْشِدْنِي وَاغْفِرْ لِي وَارْزُقْنِي مِنْ خَيْرِكَ".

   - Transliteration: "Allahumma irshidni wa ghfir li wa-rzuqni min khayrika."

   - Translation: "O Allah, guide me, forgive me, and provide me with Your goodness."

2. Dua for Mercy and Protection:
   - Dua: "اللَّهُمَّ ارْحَمْنِي وَاحْفَظْنِي مِنْ كُلِّ شَرٍّ".

   - Transliteration: "Allahumma irhamni wa ihfazni min kulli shar."

   - Translation: "O Allah, have mercy on me and protect me from all harm."

3. Dua for Sustenance and Provision:
   - Dua: "اللَّهُمَّ ارْزُقْنِي الرِّزْقَ الطَّيِّبَ وَالْبَرَكَةَ."

   - Transliteration: "Allahumma ruzuqni al-rizq al-tayyib wa al-barakah."

   - Translation: "O Allah, provide me with good sustenance and blessings."

4. Dua for Patience and Strength:
   - Dua: "اللَّهُمَّ قَوِّنِي عَلَىٰ سَعْيِي وَصَبِّرْنِي."

   - Transliteration: "Allahumma qawwini 'ala sa'yi wa sabbirni."

   - Translation: "O Allah, strengthen me in my Sa'i and grant me patience."

5. General Dua for Acceptance:
   - Dua: "اللَّهُمَّ تَقَبَّلْ عُمَرَتِي وَجَعَلْهَا خَالِصَةً لِوَجْهِكَ."

   - Transliteration: "Allahumma taqabbal 'umrati wa ja'alha khalisatan li-wajhika."

- Translation: "O Allah, accept my Umrah and make it solely for Your sake."

As you walk between Safa and Marwah, you can use these moments to reflect, make personal supplications, and seek Allah's guidance, forgiveness, and blessings. The walk itself is a time for spiritual connection and devotion.

- Duas of Supplication and Praise During Sa'i

During Sa'i, while walking between Safa and Marwah, you can recite various duas of supplication and praise. These duas help you maintain focus and devotion. Here are some recommended supplications and praises:

1. Dua for Gratitude and Praise:
   - Dua: "اللَّهُمَّ لَكَ الْحَمْدُ كَمَا يَنْبَغِي لِجَلَالِ وَجْهِكَ وَعَظِيمِ سُلْطَانِكَ".

   - Transliteration: "Allahumma laka al-hamdu kama yanbaghi lijalali wajhika wa 'azimi sultanika."

   - Translation: "O Allah, to You is due all praise as is befitting to the majesty of Your Face and the greatness of Your Authority."

2. Dua for Seeking Allah's Blessings:
   - Dua: "اللَّهُمَّ اجْعَلْنِي مِنَ الْمُبَارَكِينَ وَالْمُتَّقِينَ".

- Transliteration: "Allahumma ajilni min al-mubarakine wa al-muttaqeen."

- Translation: "O Allah, make me among those who are blessed and pious."

3. Dua for Forgiveness and Mercy:
- Dua: "اللَّهُمَّ اغْفِرْ لِي وَارْحَمْنِي وَتُبْ عَلَيَّ."

- Transliteration: "Allahumma ghfir li wa irhamni wa tub 'alayya."

- Translation: "O Allah, forgive me, have mercy on me, and turn to me in repentance."

4. Dua for Personal Needs:
- Dua: "اللَّهُمَّ قَدْ عَلِمْتُ أَنَّكَ عَلَىٰ كُلِّ شَيْءٍ قَدِيرٌ، فَاقْضِ حَاجَتِي."

- Transliteration: "Allahumma qad 'alimtu annaka 'ala kulli shay'in qadir, faqdi hajatī."

- Translation: "O Allah, I know that You are capable of everything, so fulfill my needs."

5. Dua for Strength and Patience:
- Dua: "اللَّهُمَّ قَوِّنِي وَصَبِّرْنِي وَرَزُقْنِي الصَّبْرَ عَلَىٰ طَاعَتِكَ."

- Transliteration: "Allahumma qawwini wa sabbirni wa ruzuqni al-sabr 'ala ta'atika."

- Translation: "O Allah, strengthen me, grant me patience, and provide me with endurance in Your obedience."

These duas help you remain focused on the spiritual significance of Sa'i, seeking Allah's blessings, forgiveness, and guidance throughout the ritual.

- Dua During the Jogging (Ramla) between the Green Markers

During Sa'i, the ritual of walking between Safa and Marwah includes jogging (known as Ramla) between the two green markers for men. This practice follows the example of Hagar (Hajar) and is a moment to engage in supplication. While there isn't a specific prescribed dua for this part, you can recite various supplications and praises during Ramla. Here are some recommended duas:

1. Dua for Strength and Perseverance:
   - Dua: "اللَّهُمَّ قَوِّمْ قَلْبِي وَمَنْحِي الصَّبْرَ وَالْقُوَّةَ."

   - Transliteration: "Allahumma qawwi qalbi wa manhi al-sabr wa al-quwwah."

   - Translation: "O Allah, strengthen my heart and grant me patience and strength."

2. Dua for Forgiveness and Mercy:
   - Dua: "اللَّهُمَّ اغْفِرْ لِي وَارْحَمْنِي وَتُبْ عَلَيَّ."

- Transliteration: "Allahumma ghfir li wa irhamni wa tub 'alayya."

- Translation: "O Allah, forgive me, have mercy on me, and turn to me in repentance."

3. Dua for Protection and Guidance:
- Dua: "اللَّهُمَّ احْفَظْنِي مِنَ الشَّرِّ وَالْفِتَنِ وَارْشِدْنِي."

- Transliteration: "Allahumma ihfazni min al-sharri wa al-fitani wa irshidni."

- Translation: "O Allah, protect me from harm and trials and guide me."

4. Dua for Seeking Allah's Blessings:
- Dua: "اللَّهُمَّ بَارِكْ لِي فِي سَعْيِي وَقَبِلْ عُمَرَتِي."

- Transliteration: "Allahumma barik li fi sa'yi wa qabbil 'umrati."

- Translation: "O Allah, bless my Sa'i and accept my Umrah."

5. General Praise and Supplication:
   - Dua: "اللَّهُمَّ لَكَ الْحَمْدُ وَالشُّكْرُ عَلَىٰ نِعْمَتِكَ وَفَضْلِكَ‎".

   - Transliteration: "Allahumma laka al-hamdu wa al-shukru 'ala ni'matika wa fadlik."

   - Translation: "O Allah, to You is due all praise and gratitude for Your blessings and grace."

These duas can be recited during Ramla, enhancing the spiritual experience of Sa'i and connecting you deeply with the rituals and significance of Umrah.

After completing the Sa'i ritual between Safa and Marwah, it is a meaningful time to offer supplications and seek Allah's blessings. Here are some recommended duas to recite upon completing Sa'i:

1. Dua for Acceptance and Gratitude:
   - Dua: "اللَّهُمَّ تَقَبَّلْ عُمَرَتِي وَسَعْيِي وَاغْفِرْ لِي ذُنُوبِي."

   - Transliteration: "Allahumma taqabbal 'umrati wa sa'yi wa ghfir li dhunubi."

   - Translation: "O Allah, accept my Umrah and Sa'i, and forgive my sins."

2. Dua for Blessings and Guidance:
   - Dua: "اللَّهُمَّ اجْعَلْنِي مِنَ الصَّالِحِينَ وَارْزُقْنِي مِنْ بَرَكَاتِكَ."

   - Transliteration: "Allahumma ajilni min al-salihin wa-rzuqni min barakatika."

- Translation: "O Allah, make me among the righteous and provide me with Your blessings."

3. Dua for Forgiveness and Mercy:
   - **Dua**: "اللَّهُمَّ اغْفِرْ لِي وَارْحَمْنِي وَعَافِنِي".

   - Transliteration: "Allahumma ghfir li wa irhamni wa 'afini."

   - Translation: "O Allah, forgive me, have mercy on me, and grant me health."

4. Dua for Protection and Safety:
   - Dua: "اللَّهُمَّ احْفَظْنِي مِنَ الشَّرِّ وَفِتَنِ الدُّنْيَا".

   - Transliteration: "Allahumma ihfazni min al-sharri wa fitan al-dunya."

   - Translation: "O Allah, protect me from harm and trials of this world."

5. Dua for Fulfillment of Needs:
   - Dua: "اللَّهُمَّ قَضِ حَاجَتِي وَعَافِنِي مِنْ كُلِّ ضُرٍّ".

- Transliteration: "Allahumma qadi hajatī wa 'afini min kulli durr."

- Translation: "O Allah, fulfill my needs and protect me from all harm."

These duas can be recited in gratitude for completing Sa'i and in supplication for continued blessings, forgiveness, and guidance.

- Dua of Gratitude

Offering a dua of gratitude is a beautiful way to express thanks to Allah for His countless blessings. Here is a recommended dua to recite to show your gratitude:

- Dua: "اللَّهُمَّ لَكَ الْحَمْدُ كَمَا يَنْبَغِي لِجَلَالِ وَجْهِكَ وَعَظِيمِ سُلْطَانِكَ".

- Transliteration: "Allahumma laka al-hamdu kama yanbaghi lijalali wajhika wa 'azimi sultanika."

- Translation: "O Allah, to You is due all praise as is befitting to the majesty of Your Face and the greatness of Your Authority."

Additional Duas of Gratitude

1. For Everyday Blessings:
   - Dua: "الْحَمْدُ لِلَّهِ رَبِّ الْعَالَمِينَ".

- Transliteration: "Al-hamdu lillahi rabbi al-'alamin."

- Translation: "Praise be to Allah, the Lord of all the worlds."

2. For Specific Blessings:
   - Dua: "اللَّهُمَّ شَكَرْنَاكَ عَلَىٰ نِعْمَتِكَ وَفَضْلِكَ."

- Transliteration: "Allahumma shakarnaaka 'ala ni'matika wa fadlika."

- Translation: "O Allah, we thank You for Your blessings and favor."

3. For Health and Well-being:
   - Dua: "اللَّهُمَّ لَكَ الْحَمْدُ عَلَىٰ صِحَّتِي وَعَافِيَتِي."

- Transliteration: "Allahumma laka al-hamdu 'ala sihati wa 'afiyati."

- Translation: "O Allah, to You is due all praise for my health and well-being."

4. For Spiritual Blessings:
   - Dua: "اللَّهُمَّ لَكَ الْحَمْدُ عَلَىٰ هِدَايَتِكَ وَفَضْلِكَ."

   - Transliteration: "Allahumma laka al-hamdu ‘ala hidayatika wa fadlika."

   - Translation: "O Allah, to You is due all praise for Your guidance and favor."

Reciting these duas with sincerity and gratitude helps to cultivate a sense of thankfulness and strengthens your connection with Allah.

- *Dua for Acceptance*

Seeking acceptance from Allah for your acts of worship and supplications is a profound aspect of your faith. Here is a recommended dua to ask for acceptance:

- Dua: "اللَّهُمَّ تَقَبَّلْ مِنَّا إِنَّكَ أَنتَ السَّمِيعُ الْعَلِيمُ."

- Transliteration: "Allahumma taqabbal minna innaka anta al-sami'u al-'alim."

- Translation: "O Allah, accept from us; You are the All-Hearing, the All-Knowing."

Additional Duas for Acceptance

1. General Supplication for Acceptance:
   - Dua: "اللَّهُمَّ تَقَبَّلْ عُمَرَتِي وَسَعْيِي وَاغْفِرْ لِي."

   - Transliteration: "Allahumma taqabbal 'umrati wa sa'i wa ghfir li."

- Translation: "O Allah, accept my Umrah and Sa'i, and forgive me."

2. Dua for Acceptance of Good Deeds:
   - Dua: "اللَّهُمَّ اجْعَلْ أَعْمَالَنَا خَالِصَةً لِوَجْهِكَ الْكَرِيمِ وَتَقَبَّلْهَا."

   - Transliteration: "Allahumma ja'al a'malana khalisatan li-wajhika al-karim wa taqabbalha."

   - Translation: "O Allah, make our deeds solely for Your noble Face and accept them."

3. Dua for Acceptance of Prayers and Acts of Worship:
   - Dua: "اللَّهُمَّ تَقَبَّلْ صَلَاتِي وَصِيَامِي وَسَعْيِي."

   - Transliteration: "Allahumma taqabbal salati wa siyami wa sa'i."

   - Translation: "O Allah, accept my prayers, fasting, and Sa'i."

4. Dua for Overall Acceptance:
   - Dua: "اللَّهُمَّ تَقَبَّلْ مِنَّا إِنَّكَ أَنتَ الْغَفُورُ الرَّحِيمُ."

- Transliteration: "Allahumma taqabbal minna innaka anta al-ghafur al-rahim."

- Translation: "O Allah, accept from us; You are the Forgiving, the Merciful."

Reciting these duas with sincerity and humility helps to seek Allah's acceptance of your worship and efforts.

Chapter 4:

Duas for the Final Rites of Umrah

The final rites of Umrah include important acts of worship and supplication. Here are some recommended duas to recite during these concluding moments:

1. Dua After Completing Tawaf al-Ifadah:
   - Dua: "اللَّهُمَّ اجْعَلْنِي مِنَ الَّذِينَ يُطِيعُونَكَ وَيُخْلِصُونَ لَكَ الدِّينَ."

   - Transliteration: "Allahumma ajilni min al-dhin yuti'unak wa yukhlisuna laka al-din."

   - Translation: "O Allah, make me among those who obey You and dedicate their religion solely to You."

2. Dua After Shaving or Cutting Hair:
   - Dua: "اللَّهُمَّ احْلِلْنَا مِنْ إِحْرَامِنَا وَاغْفِرْ لَنَا."

- Transliteration: "Allahumma ahillna min ihramina wa ghfir lana."

- Translation: "O Allah, release us from our state of Ihram and forgive us."

3. Dua for Protection and Forgiveness:
   - Dua: "اللَّهُمَّ احْفَظْنِي مِنَ الشَّرِّ وَاعْفُ عَنِّي."

   - Transliteration: "Allahumma ihfazni min al-sharri wa'fu 'anni."

   - Translation: "O Allah, protect me from harm and pardon me."

4. Dua for Gratitude and Acceptance:
   - Dua: "اللَّهُمَّ لَكَ الْحَمْدُ عَلَىٰ تَفْرِيجِ كُرُبِي وَتَقْبِيلِ عُمَرَتِي."

   - Transliteration: "Allahumma laka al-hamdu 'ala tafriji kurubi wa taqbil 'umrati."

   - Translation: "O Allah, to You is due all praise for relieving my distress and accepting my Umrah."

5. General Dua for Returning Home:
   - Dua: "اللَّهُمَّ ارْجِعْنِي إِلَىٰ دَارِي بِالسَّلاَمَةِ وَالْفَرَجِ".

   - Transliteration: "Allahumma raji'ni ila dari bis-salamati wa al-faraji."

   - Translation: "O Allah, return me safely to my home with ease and relief."

6. Dua for Fulfillment of Wishes:
   - Dua: "اللَّهُمَّ قَضِ حَاجَاتِي وَفِيضْ عَلَيَّ بِرَحْمَتِكَ".

   - Transliteration: "Allahumma qadi hajatī wa fidh 'alayya bi rahmatika."

   - Translation: "O Allah, fulfill my needs and shower me with Your mercy."

Reciting these duas with sincerity helps conclude your Umrah with a heart full of gratitude, seeking Allah's acceptance, protection, and guidance as you return to your daily life.

- *4.1 Duas Before Cutting Hair (Halq or Taqsir)*

Before performing Halq (shaving the head) or Taqsir (cutting a portion of the hair) during Umrah, you can recite specific duas to seek Allah's blessings and forgiveness. Here are some recommended duas:

1. Dua for Seeking Blessings and Forgiveness:
   - Dua: "اللَّهُمَّ اجْعَلْنِي مِنَ الْمُتَّقِينَ وَاغْفِرْ لِي."

   - Transliteration: "Allahumma ajilni min al-muttaqeen wa ghfir li."

   - Translation: "O Allah, make me among the pious and forgive me."

2. Dua for Completion and Acceptance:
   - Dua: "اللَّهُمَّ تَقَبَّلْ عُمَرَتِي وَحَلْقِي وَاغْفِرْ لِي."

   - Transliteration: "Allahumma taqabbal 'umrati wa halqi wa ghfir li."

- Translation: "O Allah, accept my Umrah and my shaving, and forgive me."

3. Dua for Purification and Renewal:
   - Dua: "اللَّهُمَّ طَهِّرْ قَلْبِي وَجَسَدِي."

   - Transliteration: "Allahumma tahhir qalbi wa jasadi."

   - Translation: "O Allah, purify my heart and my body."

4. Dua for Ease and Relief:
   - Dua: "اللَّهُمَّ اجْعَلْنِي مِنَ الْمُخْلَصِينَ وَأَنقِلْنِي مِنْ مَشَاقِّ السَّفَرِ."

   - Transliteration: "Allahumma ja'ilni min al-mukhlisīn wa anqilni min mashaq al-safar."

   - Translation: "O Allah, make me among the sincere and relieve me from the hardships of travel."

5. Dua for Spiritual Cleansing:

- Dua: "اللَّهُمَّ نَقِّنِي مِنَ الذُّنُوبِ كَمَا يُنَقَّى الثَّوْبُ الأَبْيَضُ مِنَ الدَّنَسِ."

- Transliteration: "Allahumma naqni min al-dhunub kama yunqa al-thawb al-abyad min al-danas."

- Translation: "O Allah, cleanse me of sins as a white garment is cleansed of dirt."

Reciting these duas helps you focus on the spiritual significance of the act, seeking Allah's blessings, forgiveness, and purification as you complete this important rite of Umrah.

- Dua for Submission and Renewal

In the final rites of Umrah, seeking Allah's submission and renewal of faith is crucial. Here's a recommended dua to recite for submission to Allah and spiritual renewal:

- Dua: "اللَّهُمَّ أَسْلَمْتُ لَكَ وَجْهِي وَفَوَّضْتُ إِلَيْكَ أَمْرِي."

- Transliteration: "Allahumma aslamtu laka wajhi wa fawwadt᾽ilayka amri."

- Translation: "O Allah, I have submitted my face to You and entrusted my affairs to You."

Additional Duas for Submission and Renewal

1. Dua for Renewal of Faith:
   - Dua: "اللَّهُمَّ جَدِّدْ إِيمَانِي وَزِدْنِي مِنْ فَضْلِكَ."

   - Transliteration: "Allahumma jaddid imani wa zidni min fadlika."

- Translation: "O Allah, renew my faith and increase me in Your favor."

2. Dua for Total Submission:
   - Dua: "اللَّهُمَّ أَسْلَمْتُ لَكَ نَفْسِي وَأَمْرِي."

   - Transliteration: "Allahumma aslamtu laka nafsi wa amri."

   - Translation: "O Allah, I submit my soul and my affairs to You."

3. Dua for Spiritual Cleansing and Guidance:
   - Dua: "اللَّهُمَّ نَقِّنِي مِنَ الذُّنُوبِ وَاهْدِنِي إِلَى الصِّرَاطِ الْمُسْتَقِيمِ."

   - Transliteration: "Allahumma naqni min al-dhunub wa hadini ila al-sirat al-mustaqim."

   - Translation: "O Allah, cleanse me of sins and guide me to the straight path."

4. Dua for Seeking Allah's Favor:
   - Dua: "اللَّهُمَّ أَكْرِمْنِي بِمَغْفِرَتِكَ وَرَحْمَتِكَ."

- Transliteration: "Allahumma akrimni bi maghfiratika wa rahmatika."

- Translation: "O Allah, honor me with Your forgiveness and mercy."

These duas help you reflect on the submission and renewal of your faith, asking Allah for guidance, purification, and an increased closeness to Him.

- 4.2 Duas After Cutting Hair (Halq or Taqsir)

After completing the ritual of cutting hair (Halq or Taqsir) during Umrah, you can recite specific duas to seek Allah's blessings, forgiveness, and acceptance. Here are some recommended duas:

1. Dua for Acceptance and Forgiveness:
 - Dua: "اللَّهُمَّ تَقَبَّلْ مِنَّا وَاغْفِرْ لَنَا."

 - Transliteration: "Allahumma taqabbal minna wa ghfir lana."

 - Translation: "O Allah, accept from us and forgive us."

2. Dua for Release from Ihram and Blessings:
 - Dua: "اللَّهُمَّ أَحِلْنَا مِنْ إِحْرَامِنَا وَبَارِكْ لَنَا."

 - Transliteration: "Allahumma ahilna min ihramina wa barik lana."

- Translation: "O Allah, release us from our Ihram and bless us."

3. Dua for Spiritual Renewal and Purification:
- **Dua**: "اللَّهُمَّ نَقِّنِي مِنَ الذُّنُوبِ وَطَهِّرْنِي".

   - Transliteration: "Allahumma naqni min al-dhunub wa tahhirni."

   - Translation: "O Allah, cleanse me from sins and purify me."

4. Dua for Gratitude and Well-being:
- Dua: "اللَّهُمَّ شَكَرْنَاكَ عَلَىٰ نِعْمَتِكَ وَعَافِنَا".

   - Transliteration: "Allahumma shakarnaaka 'ala ni'matika wa 'afina."

   - Translation: "O Allah, we thank You for Your blessings and grant us health."

5. Dua for Acceptance of Worship:
- Dua: "اللَّهُمَّ تَقَبَّلْ عُمَرَتِي وَجَزِّنِي مِنْهَا خَيْرًا".

- Transliteration: "Allahumma taqabbal 'umrati wa jazini minha khayran."

- Translation: "O Allah, accept my Umrah and reward me with goodness from it."

Reciting these duas helps conclude the ritual of cutting hair with a focus on seeking Allah's acceptance, forgiveness, and blessings, and acknowledging the completion of an important part of Umrah.

- Dua for New Beginnings

When starting a new chapter in life, whether it's after completing Umrah or embarking on any new journey, reciting a dua for new beginnings can help seek Allah's guidance, blessing, and support. Here's a recommended dua:

- Dua: "اللَّهُمَّ بَارِكْ لِي فِي بَدَائِي وَفَتَحْ لِي أَبْوَابَ الرَّحْمَةِ وَالتَّوْفِيقِ."

- Transliteration: "Allahumma barik li fi bada'i wa fath li abwaba al-rahmati wa al-tawfiqi."

- Translation: "O Allah, bless my new beginning and open the doors of mercy and success for me."

Additional Duas for New Beginnings

1. Dua for Guidance and Success:
- Dua: "اللَّهُمَّ ارْشِدْنِي إِلَىٰ خَيْرِ الْأُمُورِ وَفَتَحْ لِي أَبْوَابَ النَّجَاحِ."

- Transliteration: "Allahumma irshidni ila khayri al-umuri wa fath li abwaba al-najah."

- Translation: "O Allah, guide me to the best of matters and open the doors of success for me."

2. Dua for Blessing and Prosperity:
- Dua: "اللَّهُمَّ اجْعَلْ هَذَا الْبَدْءَ مُبَارَكًا وَفَسِّحْ لِي فِي رِزْقِي."

- Transliteration: "Allahumma ja'al hadha al-bad'a mubarakaan wa fassih li fi rizqi."

- Translation: "O Allah, make this beginning blessed and expand my provision."

3. Dua for Protection and Ease:
- Dua: "اللَّهُمَّ احْفَظْنِي مِنَ الشَّرِّ وَسَهِّلْ لِي طَرِيقَ النَّجَاحِ."

- Transliteration: "Allahumma ihfazni min al-sharri wa sahhil li tariq al-najah."

- Translation: "O Allah, protect me from harm and ease my path to success."

4. Dua for Strength and Perseverance:
   - Dua: "اللَّهُمَّ قَوِّمْ قَلْبِي وَمَنْحِنِي الصَّبْرَ وَالْقُوَّةَ".

   - Transliteration: "Allahumma qawwi qalbi wa manhi al-sabr wa al-quwwah."

   - Translation: "O Allah, strengthen my heart and grant me patience and strength."

These duas can be recited with sincerity and faith to seek Allah's blessings, guidance, and support as you embark on new endeavors.

- *4.3 Duas for Leaving Makkah*

When departing from Makkah after performing Umrah, it is a meaningful time to offer supplications for protection, blessings, and a safe journey back. Here are some recommended duas to recite:

1. Dua for a Safe Journey:
   - Dua: "اللَّهُمَّ ارْجِعْنِي إِلَىٰ دَارِي بِالسَّلاَمَةِ وَفِي أَمَانِكَ."

   - Transliteration: "Allahumma raji'ni ila dari bis-salamati wa fi amanika."

   - Translation: "O Allah, return me safely to my home and in Your protection."

2. Dua for Forgiveness and Blessings:
   - Dua: "اللَّهُمَّ اغْفِرْ لِي وَارْحَمْنِي وَبَارِكْ لِي فِي طَرِيقِي."

   - Transliteration: "Allahumma ghfir li wa irhamni wa barik li fi tariqi."

97

- Translation: "O Allah, forgive me, have mercy on me, and bless my journey."

3. Dua for Protection from Harm:
   - Dua: "اللَّهُمَّ احْفَظْنِي مِنْ كُلِّ شَرٍّ وَفِتَنٍ."

   - Transliteration: "Allahumma ihfazni min kulli sharri wa fitan."

   - Translation: "O Allah, protect me from all harm and trials."

4. Dua for Gratitude and Safe Return:
   - Dua: "اللَّهُمَّ شَكَرْنَاكَ عَلَىٰ نِعْمَتِكَ وَاجْعَلْ عَوْدَتِي بِالْسَّلاَمَةِ."

   - Transliteration: "Allahumma shakarnaaka ‘ala ni‘matika wa ja‘al ‘awdatī bis-salamati."

   - Translation: "O Allah, we thank You for Your blessings and make my return safe."

5. Dua for Sustained Guidance:
   - Dua: "اللَّهُمَّ ارْشِدْنِي وَسَدِّدْنِي فِي طَرِيقِي."

- Transliteration: "Allahumma irshidni wa saddidni fi tariqi."

- Translation: "O Allah, guide me and keep me steadfast on my path."

These duas help ensure that your departure from Makkah is accompanied by prayers for safety, protection, and continued blessings. Reciting them with sincerity can bring comfort and a sense of closure to your sacred journey.

- Dua for a Safe Return

When you are leaving Makkah and seeking a safe return to your home, reciting a dua for a safe journey and return can bring peace and reassurance. Here is a recommended dua:

- Dua: "اللَّهُمَّ ارْجِعْنِي إِلَىٰ دَارِي بِالسَّلَامَةِ وَفِي أَمَانِكَ."

- Transliteration: "Allahumma raji'ni ila dari bis-salamati wa fi amanika."

- Translation: "O Allah, return me safely to my home and in Your protection."

Additional Duas for a Safe Return

1. Dua for Protection and Safety:
- Dua: "اللَّهُمَّ احْفَظْنِي مِنَ الشَّرِّ وَأَعُوذُ بِكَ مِنْ كُلِّ سُوءٍ."

   - Transliteration: "Allahumma ihfazni min al-sharr wa a'udhu bika min kulli su."

- Translation: "O Allah, protect me from harm and I seek refuge in You from all evil."

2. Dua for Guidance and Well-being:
- Dua: "اللَّهُمَّ ارْشِدْنِي وَفَتَحْ لِي أَبْوَابَ الرَّحْمَةِ وَالْسَّلَامَةِ."

- Transliteration: "Allahumma irshidni wa fath li abwaba al-rahmati wa al-salamati."

- Translation: "O Allah, guide me and open the doors of mercy and safety for me."

3. Dua for a Smooth Journey:
- Dua: "اللَّهُمَّ سَهِّلْ لِي طَرِيقِي وَقَضِي حَاجَاتِي."

- Transliteration: "Allahumma sahhil li tariqi wa qadi hajatī."

- Translation: "O Allah, make my journey easy and fulfill my needs."

4. Dua for Gratitude and Safe Return:
- Dua: "اللَّهُمَّ شَكَرْنَاكَ عَلَىٰ نِعْمَتِكَ وَعَافِيَتِكَ وَأَمْنِى عُودَتِي."

- Transliteration: "Allahumma shakarnaaka ‘ala ni‘matika wa ‘afiyatika wa amni ‘awdatī."

- Translation: "O Allah, we thank You for Your blessings and health, and grant me security in my return."

Reciting these duas with sincerity helps seek Allah's protection and blessings for a safe and smooth return journey.

- *Dua for Future Visits to the Holy Cities*

When planning for future visits to the Holy Cities of Makkah and Madinah, it's beneficial to recite a dua asking for blessings, acceptance, and a safe journey. Here's a recommended dua for future visits:

- Dua: "اللَّهُمَّ اجْعَلْ زِيَارَتِي لِمَكَّةَ وَالْمَدِينَةِ قَبُولًا وَمُبَارَكَةً وَسَهِّلْ عَلَيَّ السَّفَرَ وَالْعِبَادَةَ."

- Transliteration: "Allahumma ja'al ziyaratī li-Makkah wa al-Madinah qaboolan wa mubarakatan wa sahhil 'alayya al-safar wa al-'ibadah."

- Translation: "O Allah, make my visit to Makkah and Madinah accepted and blessed, and ease for me the journey and worship."

Additional Duas for Future Visits

1. Dua for Safe and Blessed Journey:

- Dua: "اللَّهُمَّ احْفَظْنِي فِي رِحْلَتِي وَبَارِكْ لِي فِي زِيَارَتِي".

- Transliteration: "Allahumma ihfazni fi rihlatī wa barik li fi ziyaratī."

- Translation: "O Allah, protect me during my journey and bless my visit."

2. Dua for Acceptance of Worship:
- Dua: "اللَّهُمَّ تَقَبَّلْ عِبَادَتِي وَسَعْيِي فِي زِيَارَتِي".

- Transliteration: "Allahumma taqabbal 'ibadati wa sa'ī fi ziyaratī."

- Translation: "O Allah, accept my worship and efforts during my visit."

3. Dua for Guidance and Ease:
- Dua: "اللَّهُمَّ ارْشِدْنِي فِي سَفَرِي وَيَسِّرْ لِي زِيَارَتِي".

- Transliteration: "Allahumma irshidni fi safarī wa yassir li ziyaratī."

- Translation: "O Allah, guide me in my travel and make my visit easy."

4. Dua for Spiritual Fulfillment:
   - Dua: "اللَّهُمَّ اجْعَلْ زِيَارَتِي لِمَكَّةَ وَالْمَدِينَةِ سَبَبًا لِلتَّقَرُّبِ إِلَيْكَ."

   - Transliteration: "Allahumma ja'al ziyaratī li-Makkah wa al-Madinah sababan li-taqarrub ilayk."

   - Translation: "O Allah, make my visit to Makkah and Madinah a means of drawing closer to You."

These duas help in seeking Allah's blessings and guidance for your future visits to the Holy Cities, ensuring that your journey and worship are fulfilling and accepted.

Conclusion

As you conclude your journey through this guide to Umrah duas, it's important to reflect on the profound spiritual significance these supplications hold. The sacred journey of Umrah is not just a physical pilgrimage but a deeply transformative experience that brings you closer to Allah. Each dua, whether recited before embarking on the journey, during the rites, or upon leaving the Holy Cities, serves as a means to seek Allah's mercy, forgiveness, and blessings.

The duas for different stages of Umrah are designed to help you stay focused on the spiritual aspects of your pilgrimage. They remind you of the importance of humility, submission, and sincere worship. From preparing for the journey and performing the rituals with devotion, to seeking protection and guidance for your future visits, each prayer enhances your connection with Allah and enriches your experience.

As you return to your daily life, carry with you the essence of these prayers. Let the lessons and spirituality gained during your Umrah continue to inspire and guide you. May your sincere efforts be accepted, and may you always find strength and guidance in your faith.

Remember, the journey of faith is ongoing, and the duas you have learned are tools to help maintain your spiritual growth. Continue to turn to Allah in supplication, seek His blessings in every aspect of your life, and strive to live in a way that reflects the purity and sincerity of your pilgrimage.

May Allah accept your Umrah, grant you peace, and bless you with the opportunity to return to His sacred house again and again.

- Reflecting on the Spiritual Journey

Reflecting on the spiritual journey of Umrah is an essential part of completing the pilgrimage. This sacred journey is not merely a sequence of rites and rituals but a profound spiritual experience that reshapes your connection with Allah and enhances your faith. As you complete your pilgrimage and consider the duas you have recited, it's important to pause and reflect on the deeper meanings and impacts of your journey.

1. Renewed Faith and Devotion:

   - Umrah offers a unique opportunity to renew your faith and devotion. The process of performing acts of worship in the holy sites of Makkah and Madinah helps to rekindle your spiritual energy. Reflect on how this pilgrimage has deepened your understanding of faith and reinforced your commitment to worship.

2. Spiritual Cleansing and Transformation:

- The rites of Umrah, including Tawaf, Sa'i, and the rituals of Ihram, serve as a form of spiritual cleansing. Consider how these acts have purified your soul and transformed your inner self. Reflect on any personal growth or changes in your perspective that have occurred as a result of this journey.

3. Connection with Allah:

- The duas recited at various stages of Umrah are more than just words; they are expressions of your hopes, fears, and gratitude. Reflect on how these supplications have helped you communicate with Allah, seek His guidance, and express your deepest wishes.

4. Lessons in Humility and Patience:

- Umrah teaches valuable lessons in humility, patience, and perseverance. Reflect on the challenges you faced and how they have contributed to your spiritual growth. Consider how the experience has helped you develop a deeper sense of empathy and understanding for others.

5. Ongoing Spiritual Journey:

- The pilgrimage is a significant milestone in your spiritual journey but not the end. Reflect on how you can integrate the lessons and experiences from Umrah into your daily life. Consider how to maintain the spiritual momentum and continue to seek closeness to Allah in your everyday actions.

6. Gratitude and Future Aspirations:

- Express gratitude for the opportunity to perform Umrah and for the spiritual insights gained. Reflect on your aspirations for future visits to the holy cities and how you can strive to live a life that reflects the purity and sincerity experienced during this pilgrimage.

In conclusion, reflecting on the spiritual journey of Umrah allows you to appreciate the profound impact of this pilgrimage on your life. It's an opportunity to reaffirm your commitment to your faith, integrate the lessons learned, and continue seeking Allah's guidance and blessings in all aspects of your life. May this reflection inspire you to continue your spiritual journey with renewed dedication and sincerity.

- The Importance of Maintaining the Spirit of Umrah in Daily Life

The pilgrimage of Umrah is a deeply transformative experience that leaves a lasting imprint on your soul. However, the true essence of this journey lies not just in the rituals performed in the sacred cities, but in how the spirit of Umrah is maintained and integrated into your daily life after you return home. Here's why it's crucial to carry forward the lessons and spiritual upliftment of Umrah into your everyday existence:

1. Continuing Spiritual Growth:
   - The heightened sense of spirituality and closeness to Allah that you experience during Umrah should serve as a catalyst for ongoing spiritual growth. Incorporate regular worship, dua, and reflection into your daily routine to keep that connection strong. By doing so, you transform your everyday activities into acts of worship, fostering continuous spiritual development.

2. Living with Humility and Gratitude:

- Umrah teaches profound lessons in humility and gratitude. The simple acts of Ihram, Tawaf, and Sa'i are reminders of our equality before Allah and the blessings we often take for granted. Carrying this humility and gratitude into your daily interactions helps to maintain a balanced perspective, fostering compassion and kindness towards others.

3. Strengthening Faith and Taqwa (God-Consciousness):

- The discipline and dedication required during Umrah are essential in cultivating taqwa, or God-consciousness. By being mindful of Allah's presence in every aspect of your life, you can make decisions and live in a way that is pleasing to Him. This continuous awareness strengthens your faith and helps you to lead a life aligned with Islamic principles.

4. Practicing Patience and Perseverance:

- The challenges faced during Umrah, such as the physical exertion of the rituals and the patience required in crowded conditions, offer valuable lessons in patience and perseverance. Applying these lessons in your daily life can help you navigate personal and professional challenges with grace and resilience, knowing that these qualities are integral to your spiritual success.

5. Maintaining the Purity of Heart and Intentions:

- The purity of heart and sincerity of intentions that you cultivated during Umrah should be preserved and nurtured. Regular self-reflection and repentance (istighfar) are key to keeping your heart free from negative influences and ensuring that your actions are guided by sincere intentions.

6. Spreading the Light of Umrah to Others:

- Sharing the insights, lessons, and experiences from your Umrah with family, friends, and community members can inspire others and encourage them to embark on their spiritual journeys. This not only spreads the light of Umrah but also reinforces your commitment to maintaining its spirit.

In conclusion, maintaining the spirit of Umrah in daily life is essential for sustaining the spiritual benefits gained during the pilgrimage. By integrating the lessons of humility, patience, gratitude, and God-consciousness into your everyday actions, you can continue to grow in faith and lead a life that reflects the purity and sincerity experienced during Umrah. This ongoing commitment ensures that the spiritual journey of Umrah continues long after the physical journey has ended.

- Final Words of Encouragement and Prayer

As you conclude this journey through the Umrah guide, remember that the essence of this pilgrimage extends far beyond the rituals. The true beauty of Umrah lies in the transformation of your heart, the purification of your soul, and the deepened connection with Allah that you have nurtured.

Encouragement:

- Continue Your Spiritual Journey: The spiritual awakening you experienced during Umrah is just the beginning. Let it inspire you to continue seeking knowledge, growing in faith, and strengthening your relationship with Allah. Remember, every step you take in your daily life can be an act of worship if done with sincerity and devotion.

- Embody the Lessons Learned: Carry the humility, patience, and gratitude you've developed into your daily interactions. Let your actions be a reflection of the spiritual growth you've achieved. By living with intention and mindfulness, you can keep the spirit of Umrah alive in every aspect of your life.

- Stay Connected to the Ummah: The sense of unity and brotherhood felt during Umrah is a reminder of the strength and support that comes from being part of the global Muslim community. Continue to engage with your community, offering support, and seeking to benefit others with the knowledge and insights you've gained.

Prayer:

I pray that Allah accepts your Umrah, forgives your sins, and showers you with His infinite mercy and blessings. May He guide you on the straight path, strengthen your faith, and grant you the patience and wisdom to overcome life's challenges.

May your heart always be filled with His remembrance, and may you be granted the opportunity to return to the holy cities of Makkah and Madinah again and again. May your life be a reflection of the purity and sincerity you experienced during your pilgrimage, and may you continue to grow in love and devotion to Allah.

O Allah,

Grant us the strength to uphold the teachings of Islam in every moment of our lives. Keep us steadfast in our faith, protect us from the trials of this world, and make us among those who are constantly in Your favor. Accept our prayers, forgive our shortcomings, and bless us with the opportunity to worship You in the most beautiful of ways.

Ameen.